MW01121467

DATE DUE	RETURNED
JAN 0 2 2008	JAN 0 3 2008
FEB 1 2 2008	FEB 1 2 2008
NOV 0 3 2009	NOV 0 2 2009
NOV 2 5 2009	NOV 1 7 2009
DEC 1 4 2009	DEC 1 6 2009 DEC 0 2 2009
JAN 2 8 2010 FEB 1 2 2010	
FEB 2 6 2010 NOV 1 6 2010	MAR 1 0 2010 NOV 1 7 2010
JAN 2 5 2011	APR 0 5 2011
FEB 2 1 2012	
June 28/12	FEB 2 1 2012

Capture Me

160201

Capture Me

Judith Thompson

Playwrights Canada Press
Toronto • Canada

Playwrights Canada Press
The Canadian Drama Publisher
215 Spadina Ave. Suite 230, Toronto, Ontario CANADA M5T 2C7
416.703.0013   fax 416.408.3402
orders@playwrightscanada.com • www.playwrightscanada.com

Financial support provided by the taxpayers of Canada and Ontario through the
Canada Council for the Arts and the Department of Canadian Heritage through the
Book Publishing Industry Development Programme, and the Ontario Arts Council.

Cover photo of Maurice Dean Wint and Randi Helmers by Nir Baraket.
Cover design: JLArt
Production Editor: MZK

Library and Archives Canada Cataloguing in Publication

Thompson, Judith, 1954-
     Capture me / Judith Thompson.

A play.
ISBN 0-88754-724-9

     1. Fear--Drama. I. Title.

PS8589.H4883C36 2006   C812'.54   C2006-900027-1

First edition: May 2006.
Printed and bound by AGMV at Quebec, Canada.

I would like to dedicate this play to all the women who have been hunted down and killed by their male (ex) partners.

Capture Me was first produced at Tarragon Theatre, Toronto in January 2004 with the following company:

JERRY JOY LEE . . . . .Randi Helmers
DODGE KINGSTON . . . . .Tom McCamus
DR. DELPHINE MOTH . . . . . . .Nancy Palk
MINKLE CARLETTI . . . . .Chick Reid
AZIZ DAWOOD . . . . .Maurice Dean Wint

Directed by Judith Thompson

Set and Costume Design   Sue LePage
Lighting Design   Andrea Lundy
Music/ Sound Design   John Gzowski
Stage Management   Beatrice Campbell
                                              & Michelene Sutherland

CHARACTERS

Jerry Joy Lee, a junior kindergarten teacher, late 30s, early 40s
Dodge Kingston, Jerry's ex-husband, 50ish
Dr. Delphine Moth, Jerry's biological mother, 14 years older than
    Jerry
Minkle Carletti
Aziz Dawood, an Arabic man, late 30s, early 40s

ACT ONE

scene one

AZIZ   "What has the fine pearl to do with the world of dust? Why have you come down here? Take your baggage back. What is this place. Like the Moths of the sea, we come from the ocean, the ocean of the soul."

SFX: Sixteen children in a circle around JERRY.

JERRY   Shareefa that pink stripe is GREAT did your mom help you with that? It is beeeyootiful sweetie, uh oh give me a CRUTCH look at Ramie everybody!!! Ramie your hair is SO SWEET like candyfloss howja do that darlin? You are genius, my genius. *(big kiss)* Okay everybody let's sing the days of the week… *(She leads them in the song.)* "Sunday, Monday, Tuesday, Wednesday, Thursday, Friday, Saturdaaayyy, these are the days of the week"— GOOD morning Henrik. Hey, your hair is just the normal every day bed head did your dad forget about crazy hair day? He's going to crazy hair prison. Now, we can fix something really cool for you with my jar of dippity-doo! Of course you still have a chance for the prize, everybody has a chance for the Crazy Hair prize.

DELPHINE   Branches blossom in my body.
I breathe green leaves
across
the room

scene two

JERRY is having lunch outside.

JERRY   Hey, you, get off my shoulder. Go go go go go no, don't you come NEAR my head I just washed my hair this MORNING. Listen just because I gave you the turkey slices yesterday does NOT mean that you are getting my sandwich today—you wouldn't like avocado HEY! HEY you should be nice to me I'm one of the few humans who likes seagulls.

DODGE   Well if it isn't Geraldine Joy Lee. Talking to the birds. It is you, isn't it?

JERRY   Yes.... Yes!.... It is. Ahh.... Oh my God. It's... you...

DODGE   It's me, and it's you.

JERRY   Uh huh. Well. Hi. What are you—

DODGE   Doing here?

JERRY   I thought you lived out—west—don't you...

DODGE   I'm here now. For a while.

JERRY   Uh huh. Well.

DODGE   I thought it was you, but then I wasn't exactly sure, you're... different...

JERRY   Mmm...

DODGE   Well it has been seven years.

JERRY   Uh huh.

DODGE   We become a different person every seven years... so they say, when we shed our skin; you've put on weight, looks good on you—grown your hair, dyed your hair. I always loved the boyish auburn, this is nice you know? You were perky and gamine before, and now you are—lush. Nothing wrong with lush. So, you're ah... eating your lunch with the gulls? Like St. Francis. Hey! Still love your sandwiches— what is it, oh, avocado, soft, green, lots of vitamin E and what else are we having today? *(She covers up her food.)* I'm sorry, I remember how private you are... about your food, secret eating, oh I remember catching you at four in the morning with your head in the fridge, a cold potato in your mouth. HEY! *(to a gull)* Get out of here! Go on! The lake is that way! Yeah. You are lush and—Dazzling, actually. You are dazzling me with your lusciousness.

JERRY   I... should really get going, it's almost...

DODGE	And HOW ARE YOU? Are you as well as you LOOK?
JERRY	I'm fine. *(beat)* And how are you?
DODGE	Oh I'm great, just great Jerry... better than I have ever been, actually, I'm on a leave of absence; here to teach a group of—damaged adolescents, well, really, juvenile delinquents, you know, kids serving time in jail for anything you can think of... shooting corner store clerks to death for a pack of cigarettes, stabbing their girlfriends in the eye, burning down their houses. Apparently whoever's in charge thought my kind of popular philosophy would, ah... stimulate, or... soothe these savage boy monsters—I—I have to say, I was hoping I would run into you. I have thought about you... quite a lot, actually, over the years. And I don't know maybe you have thought about me it's only natural, I don't understand these people who were married to someone for twenty years and then claim they never think of them as if they have erased their past, you know? You can't ERASE the past, it's written into your body. So what are you doing these days. Did you ever go to—cooking school, or—
JERRY	No.
DODGE	Oh that's too bad. You had a bit of flair in the kitchen I loved that dish you used to make, the artichoke hearts smothered in... what did you used to smother them in? *(beat)* DOG GROOMING, that's it, you were going to open a...
JERRY	That was not really serious.
DODGE	You used to do an excellent job on our neighbours' labradoodle, Lacy; How about the whole Christian thing are you still religious?
JERRY	In my quiet way.
DODGE	You used to love your Jesus, you still go to church? Sing in the choir?
JERRY	Sometimes.

DODGE	Still a believer, huh?
JERRY	I'm sorry, I really do have to get back.
DODGE	*(He sits.)* JERRY JOY. God. What are the chances of running into you in a city of four million, eh? Remember how we used to argue about destiny?
JERRY	Mmm.
DODGE	You believed it was unavoidable.
JERRY	No.
DODGE	Yes.... Well. It couldn't be a more glorious day, could it? A bright song of a day. So, what is it exactly that you do?
JERRY	I... work for the city.
DODGE	Do you landscape its parks or pick up its garbage or patrol its streets or promote its landmarks what is it that you DO?
JERRY	Ohh, just... this and that.
DODGE	Still this-ing and that-ing. I don't know if you heard, I got married. To a lovely girl, her name is Leanne.
JERRY	Oh. That's nice.
DODGE	We've got four daughters, do you believe it?
JERRY	Four? You have...
DODGE	I know. Me and all these wonderful females. It's hilarious.
JERRY	Congratulations.
DODGE	Thanks; Life is fantastic; What about you, you married?
JERRY	Listen, I—
DODGE	Dating anyone?

JERRY   I um... I really REALLY have to get back to work now.

DODGE   Oh. Oh I'm SORRY, I do blunder on. So, where is it you said you work?

JERRY   Just... I really have to get back. It was... nice to see you.

DODGE   Yeah. REALLY nice to see you, Jerr. Seeing you makes me ring like a bell inside, to be honest I... I don't know, sometimes, I'm walking along the street, I see... like... an old dog hobbling along and I'll think Jerr would have LOVED that dog, cause you always did have a huge heart. Let me give you my card, I'll be here for a few months, call me anytime.

She takes his card.

JERRY   I'm late. I'm sorry, I'm really late.

DODGE   You white rabbit, you. HEY. Shall we get together for lunch this week? I know this brilliant place by the water where they bring everything to your table on fire!

JERRY   Sure, maybe, I don't know, I'll have to...

DODGE   GREAT to see you again! And I know it's great for your heart, I can hear it beating!

scene three

AZIZ speaks to an unseen Immigration Officer.

AZIZ   Each seed has an embryo in it and the embryo grows into the plant first the roots, then the stem, and when the stem grows the seed coat of the seed falls off. And then comes the leaves and then the flower and it needs water, air, space and sun to grow. And then it can grow on its own. All on its own.

Was difficult to get books. Our village was very far... far from—

I can talk about plants, Sir. About the life of a seed, a seed embryo; this is what I was teaching to the children on the day that...

It is written on the paper. Surely you can understand my reluctance to to—speak—after that happened I could not speak for months.

You think I am lying? Because I do not have a missing leg? Or a wound from a knife...

If I speak... about what happened, Mister Officer of Immigration, I will... I will lose my power of speech. I need to speak to drive a taxi here, to make a living for my daughter. To save money to bring over my sister and her children. Can you understand? I cannot speak the words.

You are going to force me to...?

They are all dead. All of my family.

I am dead. Or almost dead and in a last dream a final desperate dream of seeking... refuge in your beautiful and bleak and unending.... Will you welcome me to your country? Or will you turn me away?

scene four

DODGE teaches.

DODGE   Did ja see that eclipse last night? HOLY SHIT it was like the end of the world or the beginning of a new even STRANGER one than this one if that's possible. Eh? Eh? Now listen, I know you guys have been forced to take this class, you're thinking pain in the ass it's a punishment, a bad tasting medicine, but I'm gonna try my best to make it sweet, make it sizzle even, because I'll tell you, I am really happy, no thrilled to be here with you, it is my golden... privilege... to be your guide because you know

why? Because every goddamned one of you is
a genius. Oh yes, I mean it, don't doubt it I know,
I know you've been told that you're trouble, you're
stupid you're worthless, but in every one of you,
there is a universe, there is music in your voices,
there is art in your souls, in your eyes there is
vision. Every one of you oh yes is possessed of pure
ringing singing genius, believe it. It may only flow
out for one minute of your life, it may flow out for
years, maybe your moment of genius is so long ago
you can't remember it, maybe it was a terrible
moment for you because genius is not always
cuddle by no means but we all have it, roiling
around in us somewhere our secret stream of
genius—and what is it? It is the moment when each
of us transcends our human-ness when we become
part of a much more powerful immortal force; like
most of you… a natural disaster. We become GOD
we become the Devil we become the spring warmth
melting the snow we become…. The volcano erupts,
the earth quakes, the tornado lifts the tractor-trailer
into the sky and tears apart the well constructed
house.

Today we are going to talk about your genius.

scene five

JERRY   FOUR DAUGHTERS. He has FOUR DAUGHTERS.

MINKLE   So. Ya see? He's not a threat, how could a man with
four daughters be a threat to anyone?

JERRY   When I left him he said he would give me seven
years of freedom and then he would come and
he would carve my heart out, like those teenage
soldiers in Sierra Leone. *(beat)* It's been seven years,
exactly.

MINKLE   Hah. Well that's about as scary as Mr. Bean at
a bank machine. Come off it.

JERRY   Minky you don't know how crazy he is.

MINKLE   Joyo you're a paranoid drama queen. Your life is boring; you're a boring, sunny side up JK teacher whose biggest achievement is making pink Valentine's day cupcakes, you're looking for the knife edge. For Christ sake he was passing by the school he saw you in the park.

JERRY   Oh no. No. Minkle, he's come for me. And he means to kill me.

MINKLE   *(beat)* But he is married, with four gals, his own little kingdom back there. He doesn't need you.

JERRY   There was something insane behind his eyes, his voice. Minkle, this happens every day, read the paper it's not only bouncers and carpet cleaners who kill their girlfriends and wives you know, it's EVERY kind of…

MINKLE   Jerry. Maybe you WANT someone to be obsessed with you.

JERRY   Are you saying you don't believe me?

MINKLE   I believe in what I can see, hear, touch and smell. Practical Patty, always have been. I don't know, Jerr. Nothing is as weird as it seems. Just stop, drop and roll and put out your paranoid fires.

JERRY   I know I am in mortal danger—

MINKLE   Jerry. Don't say that. Don't EVER say that to me unless you are totally 300 percent positive. *(beat)* Would you give me a pedicure tonight? Whatshisname is complaining about my toenails scraping him. Come on, we'll get out the loofah, the lotion, put on the coffeepot.

JERRY   As soon as I saw him I felt like a rag doll, without any—

MINKLE   OH piffle. Piffle whiffle stop your whining. Oh jeez I'm going to need a STRONG coffee tonight. I gotta be up all night talking to Ray.

JERRY   What's wrong with Ray?

MINKLE	He's depressed, my new sister-in-law won't sleep with him and he's going blind from diabetes. *(beat)*
JERRY	You know how I tracked down my biological mother a few years ago—
MINKLE	In a moment of very sloppy sentiment.
JERRY	—but never actually called her or anything?
MINKLE	Because I forbade you.
JERRY	I have this overwhelming yearning to—
MINKLE	Whaddya think, she's gonna ride in on a white horse with a silver sword? Forget about it, baby. *(beat)* You know? I'm the only person I know without a single problem. It's like, we're all in the water, and I'm the one on the nice sturdy raft and everyone around me, screaming, drowning. It's like "Get offa my raft, and I'll throw you a lifejacket, but you're not getting on my raft." Well. Maybe you can. *(beat)* Listen. I really don't think you have anything to worry about.
	I know that particular nightmare. I've smelled it up close. And this? Doesn't smell like that.

scene six

AZIZ with SHARZIA, reading Green Eggs and Ham *(by Dr. Seuss) at bedtime.*

AZIZ	You see Sharzia? The funny little creature man wants the larger Sam I Am to eat his green eggs and ham.
	I don't know. Why do you think? No. We do not have green eggs in our country but it is perhaps something they have here. We will ask Mrs. Tetra about it tomorrow when she comes to show us your new school. No. No you will not be forced to eat green eggs and ham.

Yes, tomorrow you will go to school—new school
with lots of nice girls and boys—no no no of course
they will play with you no, no, they will never
know that! No. They will never know. Well. We will
tell them that Momma is on a big, happy boat in the
sea, and that one day, she will be here. Sleep Now.

scene seven

Phone ringing.

DELPHINE Hello, Dr. Delphine Moth here. Hello, who is calling
please? Hello? Helloooo. Hello? Oh dear me I do
not have time for a heavy breather; not tonight, you
poor hungry soul.

*DELPHINE and JERRY hang up, simultaneously
touching their ears.*

scene eight

DODGE teaches.

DODGE Who here in this room believes in EVIL?

Now a lot of people out there in the world would
say that you are evil. After all, you're all servin time
for something, right? You are the criminal element,
the reason they're afraid of the dark. They read
about the things ya did in the paper, they think
you're the devil; I've read through your files,
a couple of you killed a taxi driver for the forty
bucks in his box, he was a father of seven, some
of you robbed corner stores and beat up the cashier,
or shot her through the groin, left her paralyzed
one of you killed a cop, hey, don't look alarmed
everything's out in the open here, that's what this
is ABOUT that is why you are here some of you
have done horrifying things to other boys your age
and I won't even start on what a few of you have
done to the young ladies in your lives.

Evil is like a riptide, huh? Like a current you can't fight, isn't it? Isn't it? And every one of you got pulled way out to the middle of the dark sea didn't you? It's real dark out there. And there is no moon to light your way there is NOTHING.

And you're probably asking yourself "What was that?" "Like, what the fuck happened there? THAT was not ME, I'm a nice guy, I'm even a sweet guy, I like kids, LOVE my grandmother, take my cat to the vet's, write poems for my girlfriend, what the fuck was that running through my blood?"

It wasn't you. You are good guys. Inside. You are human beings. Human beings who were in a life and death struggle with "Radical Evil!" Sounds like something outside of us, doesn't it? Like a hurricane, like poison gas, like an animal like "the devil made me do it" but the scary thing is is that Radical Evil is within US. It is us. Within you and me and every human being on this earth in fact EVIL is what MAKES us human.

scene nine

JERRY, AZIZ. Junior Kindergarten Room. Evening.

AZIZ   Good evening. I am father to Sharzia. Aziz Dawood.

JERRY   Jerry Joy Lee. Hello it's very nice to meet you.

AZIZ   I am early?

JERRY   You're PERFECT; a few parents didn't show up, so—

AZIZ   I am father to Sharzia.

JERRY   Yes! Yes, of course, her babysitter, Yasmeen, usually brings her oh we LOVE Sharzia; wouldja like to sit down?

AZIZ   Thank you.

JERRY   Well.

AZIZ	I must have a babysitter because I am working at three jobs right now; it is necessary.
JERRY	Oh, I understand.
AZIZ	Taxi, night cleaning office, and pizza delivery.
JERRY	I have many parents in that situation.
AZIZ	I was teacher in my country.
JERRY	WELL! You'll have to come in and talk to the kids about your country.
AZIZ	No.
JERRY	Oh, of course, if you—
AZIZ	I try to see her two hours per day. To read her a story in English and in our language every night. We say our morning prayers and our evening prayers.
JERRY	That is fantastic!
AZIZ	She is learning well?
JERRY	Oh yes. Would you like to see some of her work?
AZIZ	Yes.
JERRY	I have her whole portfolio here for you, Mr. Dawood. Look at that, that is a picture of a garden, she wanted me to write, "My mother's garden has happy birds and pretty red flowers but watch out for the black snake in the corner." And look at this, she is writing her name VERY well for junior kindergarten. Shall I call you Mr. Dawood? Or Aziz? I'm kind of a first name person.
AZIZ	Aziz, of course, you may call me Aziz. Oh. She draws this figure well, I think.
JERRY	Yes. Oh yes she does. Well I will call you Aziz then, and you call me…
AZIZ	You are Miss Joy. A fortunate name, I think.

JERRY	Lee, actually. Jerry Joy Lee. My father? Was Chinese. Of Chinese Ancestry. I was… adopted.
AZIZ	I have come to tell to you—a secret about my daughter;
JERRY	Yes?
AZIZ	She may be… frightened of certain things.
JERRY	The national anthem. She hides, in the washroom.
AZIZ	Because. Perhaps because… of the…
JERRY	Unspeakable events… that… led to… your leaving your country and…?
AZIZ	—and knocking on the door of your country.

AZIZ smiles and knocks, JERRY follows suit. They laugh.

scene ten

MINKLE with parent.

MINKLE	Mrs. Johanson I'm gonna be straight with you your daughter is a bully. Eight years old and sweet as pie to the adults and as soon as we turn around she turns this class into her very own torture chamber. Oh yes, I know she's tiny don't think that slows her down a bit, she gets the bigger kids to be her goons, she has a nose for the more fragile children, the children whose parents are going through divorce, the children who come to school with bruises, or faces swollen with tears she goes right for the throat with those kids, has lots of fun turning everyone else against them too.

Your child is a psychopath. And if she doesn't get some serious help RIGHT AWAY she is going to go through her life like a tornado, destroying everything in her sweet little path.

MINKLE, JERRY:

MINKLE	Oh my Christ in a kerchief these parents.
JERRY	Yeah?
MINKLE	"My husband, who is a Vice President of the Scotia Bank believes that you marked that science project unfairly. We both worked very hard with Daniel." So I go "YOU did it ya buffalo." This other one, she says her kid is scared of me, cause I talk too fast and too mean. I say what are you talkin about the kids LOVE me, I'm a fast talker, she says I should slow-right-down, she's a fucking child psychologist, and she says practice, right now—I go "Fuuuuuck youuuu." She goes "I'm reporting your vulgarity to the principal," I say, "go right a fucking head he's my boyfriend."
JERRY	I just fell in love.
MINKLE	WHAT?
JERRY	With the handsomest man I have ever seen in my entire life.
MINKLE	Where is he?
JERRY	Like a hurricane inside my—
MINKLE	Uh oh when you start with the poetry corner I'm out the door, dear. Goodbye. See ya at Freaky Fridays.
JERRY	WAIT. Minkle. I really think I'm in love. For the first time ever. I have never felt anything like this!
MINKLE	So did you hit on him?
JERRY	NO! Well, in a way.
MINKLE	What's his first language?
JERRY	Why do you ask?
MINKLE	Well.
JERRY	I don't know. Not English.
MINKLE	That's good.

JERRY   Why?

MINKLE   Because. Then he won't realize what a looloo you
            are.

          JERRY makes up a love song.

JERRY   Love… has got me like the lightning gets the TREE.
            Ooooh oh happy me… no grey days, no PMS no oh
            poor me because I'MMM the happy TREE see the
            bluebirds a singin' on MEEEE see my blossoms
            bloomin' on two three see LOOOOOve has got me
            like the LIGHTNING gets the tree… I am the happy
            MEEEEEEEEEE…

DODGE   *(a memory—JERRY stops singing)* You can leave me,
            love, that's absolutely fine. You are a free agent
            I have never for a minute felt that I owned you.
            Seven wonderful years of marriage, it's been a gas,
            it's been a beautiful ride. A sensual, spiritual aurora
            borealis.

          JERRY begins the song again, under DODGE'S
          speech: "Love has got me like the lightning gets the
          tree…"

            I mean, who can own a human being? You are not
            a dog or a pet turtle; go! Move on! Be free. I will
            miss your charming laugh, your curious mind, your
            passion for lemons, just remember, lovelamb, that
            a day will come, a day when you are utterly content
            as a daffodil in a warm breeze and the air will
            CRACK *(JERRY abruptly stops singing.)* and nothing
            will ever be the same.

MINKLE   So I guess this is the first time you've ever felt like
            this, huh?

JERRY   Yeah.

MINKLE   So now you know why I have been with Francis for
            sixteen years. Even though he will be married till
            the day he dies and I'm his every other Wednesday
            fucking Geisha and—I hate—the ground the man
            walks on; I feel the way you feel. He pats me on the

head he tickles my belly and I'm on my back in
adoration.

JERRY   ADORATION.

MINKLE   Yeah, Like a nun, breathless with adoration.

scene eleven

*At home. DELPHINE is dancing and singing the
same tune as JERRY.*

DELPHINE LOOOOOVE has got me like the LIGHTNING gets
the TREE like rolling thunder clapping ONE TWO
THREE—like rolling thunder clapping ONE TWO
THREE oh LOVE SAYS— *(DELPHINE answers the
phone.)*

Hello Dr. Delphine Moth here. Hello? Hello? Who is
this? Is this Mrs. Shabot? Are you alright dear?

Did you have a seizure and you're having difficulty
speaking? Now don't feel badly about calling in the
middle of the night I was working anyway, love, so
just.... Who is calling please? Are you a patient of
mine? Oh I see. It's you. The prankster, again, are
you playing a PRANK dear? Having a giggle at my
expense are you? Listen, whoever you are, whether
you are a gaggle of teenyboppers or a pathetic
pervert in a bad brown suit I am a person, here,
on the other end, working hard. I have a life and
I would like to warn you if you call me again I will
have your call traced and you will look up and see
police officers with big guns and handcuffs nobody
messes with Dr. Delphine nobody!

*Both DELPHINE and JERRY hang up quickly.
Both touch their ears.*

And what is that trickling from my ear? I haven't
been swimming since last summer.

scene twelve

Junior Kindergarten Room, AZIZ and JERRY.

AZIZ	Please. I don't understand. *(He shows her something.)*
JERRY	This is…. Oh. This is an invitation; to Brianna's birthday party.
AZIZ	Fifth birthday party. Saturday… two to five. 156 Roxton Avenue. Please. Is it required to bring something?
JERRY	Well, a little gift is usually—
AZIZ	A little gift?
JERRY	Oh… oh not an expensive one, that would embarrass them, just a trinket.
AZIZ	A trinket?
JERRY	A little toy, you know,—five or ten dollars.
AZIZ	*(He writes.)* Five or ten dollars. What please, what is appropriate gift?
JERRY	Oh anything, a teddy bear, a dolly, a book.
AZIZ	*(He writes.)* Teddy bear, dolly book. What is appropriate to wear, please?
JERRY	Well. Something nice, but not too nice.
AZIZ	What does this mean?
JERRY	Well… some of them just wear the kind of thing they wear to school, others put on a little dress, and tights.
AZIZ	She will wear her very special dress. From my country.
JERRY	It's not necessary—after all, you won't want to get it dirty.
AZIZ	That is not important. What is important is to say thank you for invitation, for kindliness to my

daughter. My daughter she is very excited about the birthday party. Very happy. She will wear beautiful very beautiful dress.

JERRY   Sure… why not.

AZIZ   Is it necessary for me to dress in a shirt, a tie, suit jacket? Western suit?

JERRY   OH No, no just casual, the parents are very casual. Jeans, whatever.

AZIZ   Is it expected that I stay with her?

JERRY   No, oh no no. Most parents want you to leave. I mean you can stay if you want, but it's not expected.

AZIZ   I will wait outside. On the porch.

JERRY   Oh no, no just go off and—

AZIZ   I will not leave her. What if somebody kidnap my daughter, take her away, to Florida?

JERRY   That won't happen. And it just… doesn't look right to wait on the porch. They'll think there is something wrong with you.

AZIZ   And what shall I do for three hours?

JERRY   Whatever. Go for a walk. Wash the car.

AZIZ   This is not easy to learn.

JERRY   I know.

AZIZ   And what will they do at the fifth birthday party? Will they play games she must learn? That will frighten her. She will cry out for me.

JERRY   But they would teach her right there. Don't worry, Mr. Dawood, she'll be fine. Just… pin the tail on the donkey.

AZIZ   No.

JERRY   Oh. Alright, I'll talk to the mother.

AZIZ	Yes please. And will there be this sweet food called birthday cake?
JERRY	Oh yes.
AZIZ	And is there meat in this cake? She cannot eat meat. *(JERRY laughs.)* Why are you laughing?
JERRY	Because, the idea of a meat cake, I don't know.
AZIZ	You have meat pie, why not a meat cake?
JERRY	It just… isn't a thing.
AZIZ	I think there is meat in the cake because I asked at the Loblaw's food market what was in the sweet spreading and the old woman said beef tallow. That is fat from a cow. There is meat in your cake.
JERRY	Well. Hm. You got me there.
AZIZ	I beg your pardon?
JERRY	You are correct. She doesn't have to eat the cake. She could just have the ice cream. She's going to be fine, Aziz, she'll love it. Little kids LOVE birthday parties.

Silence while he looks through the drawings.

AZIZ	Miss Geraldine? What else is my daughter afraid of?
JERRY	Scissors.
AZIZ	Yes.
JERRY	Screaming?
AZIZ	Yes.
JERRY	The bell.
AZIZ	Yes. I try to explain to her.
JERRY	She cries. Every time it rings. She runs to me and I just hold her. Sing to her: *(from* Love you Forever *by Robert Munsch)* "I'll love you forever, I'll like you

for always, as long as I'm living my baby you'll be…"

AZIZ   Thank you. She has no mother… to…

JERRY   I'm so sorry.

AZIZ   Yes. I am sorry, too.

JERRY   Yes.

AZIZ   Yes. You are good to my daughter. Thank you.

JERRY   I… I can understand her fears, Mr. Dawood.

AZIZ   How is it, Miss Lee, that you understand her fears?

JERRY   Well I…

AZIZ   I think you are an excellent teacher for my daughter.

JERRY   I really love your daughter, Mr. Aziz.

AZIZ   I thank you. For loving my daughter. I thank you very much. Miss Jerry Joy Lee.

scene thirteen

DELPHINE opens a letter, reads it:

DELPHINE   "Outside my night window
A pear tree
Four stories high
Breaks through the glass
Branches cover my bedclothes
And blossom in my cold body
I breathe green leaves across the room
The wind is with me

All I need to be
Is the green mother
Pear tree
Onliest Aloneliest
The wind is with me
Green mother pear tree.
The wind is with me."

No return address. Do I have a "stalker"? Perhaps he and his friends have watched me washing and dancing by myself, one breasted woman in the window, night after night. Perhaps they are sneering and making vomiting sounds when they see me. God, I had better order bars for the window. Ductal Carcinoma in situ. Like rust. Why would anybody watch a woman with one breast?

scene fourteen

JERRY faces AZIZ, but hears MINKLE behind her.

MINKLE	So he's not the dating type so teach him some English grammar.
JERRY	I will have been fed.
MINKLE	Listen, if he wants to move up in the world he has to master the lingua franca, baby. So set up some lessons, what about the future perfect?
AZIZ	I will have been fed… after I have my evening dinner.
MINKLE	That's a cute tense.
JERRY	Well. Sort of—
AZIZ	The future is perfect.
JERRY	More like… I will have been fed… by… nine o'clock. Or, no, more like, "When I meet my mother, I will have been…" no.
MINKLE	After I have sex I will have been fuck—
JERRY	—NO! It's… like… imagining or… projecting, you know? Projecting the future—like, next Sunday, I will have been teaching you English for—
AZIZ	Four weeks.
JERRY	Yes! Yes that's it!
AZIZ	Future perfect.

JERRY	Yes.
AZIZ	I will have been learning from an excellent teacher for four weeks.
JERRY	Thank you.
AZIZ	I will have been... thank-ful...
JERRY	No.
AZIZ	Yes.
JERRY	NO. I will have been thankful, for you...
AZIZ	No.
JERRY	Kindness.
AZIZ	Your... kindness.
JERRY	And your voice. I don't know. Your voice.
AZIZ	My voice.
JERRY	A beautiful...

JERRY takes his hand.

Is this okay?

He is embarrassed. She withdraws her hand.

I'm sorry. I'm so sorry.

He takes her hand back, and hungrily holds it to him, chastely. He turns away. Leaves.

AZIZ	Goodbye. Thank you for the lesson in future perfect.

scene fifteen

DELPHINE on the phone.

DELPHINE	Do you think it's anything to worry about Officer? There have been three calls and one letter, containing a—poem. No, nothing overtly lewd.

But frightening nonetheless. Every time I leave the house I am as nervous as a wet hen, and if a car so much as slows down near me I nearly have a cardiovascular incident my sister tells me I'm a nervous nelly, and I probably am, oh yes, yes, you're right I'm sure it will stop, of course, yes, of course, I am somewhat alarmist, I know. Thank you Officer, I am dreadfully sorry to take up your time. You all do a wonderful job for us. Good night then. You sleep well now. *(She hangs up.)* Oh I suppose he won't be sleeping if he's working now; stupid me. Stupid, stupid me.

scene sixteen

JERRY, leaving the supermarket.

DODGE   Remember that scene in Othello?

JERRY gasps.

The scene with Othello and Iago, where Iago finally convinces Othello that Desdemona is a cheating whore.

JERRY   Dodge? What are you doing here?

DODGE   Looking for you.

JERRY   I will get a restraining order.

DODGE   I saw you with your lover, walking hand in hand, laughing, kissing, right on the street; Your foreign love—So, I don't know if you remember, but he explodes with this most wonderful phrase, full of real muscular intention, "I will tear her all to pieces." So simple. Lupine.

JERRY   Dodge. You are married with four daughters.

DODGE   They're always asking about you; "Why doesn't Aunt Jerry ever come by, you talk so much about her, Dad."

JERRY   Come off it, Dodge.

l to r: Randi Helmers, Tom McCamus
photo by Nir Baraket

DODGE   So does he speak to you in his language when he—
         ravishes you? You know that he has nothing but
         contempt for you; In his culture loose women like
         you are nothing but prostitutes. So how many
         lovers have ya had since you left me, twenty, thirty,
         five hundred?

         And when a body has no breath, does it have no
         grace? What do you think?

JERRY   If you are trying to scare me, it's working, okay? I'm
         scared, look, my hands are shaking. Now go away
         please, just... go... home.

DODGE   I'm not going home, before I have your grace—

JERRY   My grace?

DODGE   —You really don't understand, do you?

JERRY   You are mentally ill and you need help.

DODGE	Oh—Leanne sends her love, I talked to her last night! And the girls are still reading the box set of *Emily of New Moon (by L.M. Montgomery)* books you didn't send a few years ago so come on, dish! How is the sex with your new lover? Is it better than it was with me?
JERRY	Is that what this is about?
DODGE	What what is about?

Silence.

	So. See you at the park, around 12:30? We'll have a great old chat. Maybe you'll even let me put my arm around you Jerr? Or come in your face? I'd like that.
JERRY	Oh my God.
DODGE	So, 12:30. That okay? You don't have anything else on, do you?
JERRY	How long do I have, Dodge? Can you at least tell me that?
DODGE	Oh Good God. Geraldine none of us can know that, can we? Can anyone know that?

DODGE alone—he takes three deep breaths. Exit.

scene seventeen

MINKLE	"I will tear her all to pieces."
JERRY	Yeah! My heart is all over the place.
MINKLE	That's arrhythmia. Nothing to worry about. Just lie down flat till it goes away. My mother has it. So does my aunt. Hearts like, instead a boombum boombum boom bum it boomboom BOOM nothing to worry about.
JERRY	And I don't sleep at all anymore.

MINKLE   (*beat*) What about the police? They're actually really good on this thing now.

JERRY   Ha. Ha ha ha ha.

MINKLE   What about Aziz? He's like your very own army for fuck's sake.

JERRY   No.

MINKLE   Why not?

JERRY   What Aziz and I have is pure. It's all about Sharzia and poetry and here and now. I don't ask him anything about his other life and he doesn't ask me either.

MINKLE   I know, make friends with that Satan's Choice guy down the street, Joey, give him a blowjob or something.

> *Beat.*

JERRY   I wonder how he is going to tear me to pieces. With his bare hands? Or with some kind of…

MINKLE   Listen, if it comes to that, we'll just take right off. We'll drive all the way to Come by Chance Newfoundland; we'll start a school for fisher-children, we'll have a ball. We will do what we have to do.

JERRY   I do have just this sliver of hope.

MINKLE   Hope is a fucking mirage.

scene eighteen

MINKLE   Hey.

> *DODGE turns around.*

YOU are a fucking creep.

DODGE   Excuse me?

MINKLE	You heard what I said.
DODGE	I think... you must be mistaking me for someone else.
MINKLE	You here waiting for Jerry to get home, so you can INTIMIDATE her or worse aren't you?
DODGE	Not at all, I am on my way to Massey Lecture Hall, for a talk.
MINKLE	What talk.
DODGE	It's listed in the paper.
MINKLE	Are you or are you not hunting down my friend?
DODGE	What do you think?
MINKLE	I think you are. I know you are.
DODGE	Mmm mm. Nothing like the zeal of the converted. How well do you know Jerry?
MINKLE	Extremely well. She's one of my girls, she's my best girl in fact.
DODGE	Listen. Jerry is a dear sweet woman, she has a child's pure soul but... she has fears.
MINKLE	She told me about the marriage. The horRENdous abuse.
DODGE	Ohhh Geraldine. You know she was diagnosed as bi-polar when she was twenty. Did she not tell you that? Check her medicine cabinet. Oh yes, SEVERE manic depressive and pathological liar, don't tell me you haven't caught her countless little lies.
MINKLE	Well, we all... tell little polka dotty.
DODGE	What she had for lunch, where she grew up, how many sisters and brothers, what colour her phone is, she can't stop. You've probably accepted it, as part of her nature, you don't even call her on them anymore, right?

MINKLE   But stupid little lies are a very far cry from... from the NIGHTMARES that YOU...

DODGE   She always had... nightmares. About a tree, about being tied to it. Terrible nightmares, maybe they stemmed from something in her childhood her parents were religious fanatics she has mixed up the nightmares with... her life. With her OWN history. Does that make any sense?

MINKLE   You are saying that Jerry has mixed up her dreams with—

DODGE   Haven't you ever had a dream so real so very real that when you wake up you are convinced that it was real, or at least had real meaning?

MINKLE   Yes. All the time.

DODGE   We all do. And yet... there is something seductive... last night I dreamt there was a man with three swords chasing me through libraries, and I had to turn out all the lights in the library, so he wouldn't see me, and it was terrifying, terrifying, but when I woke up, I wanted to go back. To the world of the dream.

MINKLE   What is that?

DODGE   Well. A dream is the disguised fulfillment of an unconscious wish.

MINKLE   Okay, if you say so.

DODGE   I'm sorry, I hope you don't mind me saying this, but you are an.... Inspiring woman.

MINKLE   What?

DODGE   A true friend; seriously cynical, yet wide open to new thought, unique and... ravishing.

MINKLE   Ravishing.

DODGE   You are flowing into my veins and I am helpless. I honestly, truly, have never even had a harsh thought about Jerr. I hope you believe me, because you—

MINKLE   I... don't know. When I'm with her, I believe her. But... now...

DODGE   Where there is doubt, there is freedom.

MINKLE   Shit. SHIT.

> *DODGE caresses MINKLE, she falls into his arms.*

DODGE   ...I have a hotel room.

MINKLE   We don't need a hotel room. Look at all the snow, it is melting for us, melting away, God, vanishing let us just fall into the melting...

> *DODGE disappears, MINKLE wakes up.*

Holy Shit. What a fucking nightmare. Except it's weird. I kinda want to go back. I kind of actually want to go back there. Don't tell anybody. Minkle, don't tell any of your girls they will never respect you again. Don't even tell your shrink.

JERRY   *(to MINKLE)* I had this dream? That you betrayed me.

MINKLE   No way.

JERRY   With Dodge. He he... seduced you. Right in the park, in the snow. And I'm there watching...

MINKLE   Dreams are so fried.

scene nineteen

DODGE   Alright you alligators let us talk about love.

Sex. The WILD thing.

Gentlemen. Every one of you is, at heart, a gentleman. Every one of you has an innocent side. Sometimes finding that side is like kissing your elbow, but I KNOW that it is there. Like the

three of you who put together these slides for me.
Cole, Devon, Jeremy what a fine job you did. I look
at you and I see the perfect little boys that you once
were. Perfectly sweet to your mothers, you sisters;
See, the trouble is, we need them. We NEED the fair
sex, not just because we need sex, but because they
civilize us, don't they? They make us better people.
Gentler people. We can talk to them, confide in
them in a way we can't talk to our guy friends, our
colleagues. We NEED them. And that pisses us off,
doesn't it? And so we are sometimes unfair to the
women in our lives, we are sometimes even...
brutal.

Aren't you? AREN'T YOU, YOU BASTARDS?

How many of you wear a condom during sex?

How many of you ignore your lady when she asks
you to put one on? Uh huh. And you usually get
your way, don't you? And sometimes, she gets
knocked up. Yes? And sometimes, she has an
abortion, and you breathe a sigh of relief, and
sometimes, she keeps the baby. And you RUN.
And if you do see her on the street with the kid
in the stroller, you pretend you don't know her.
Because you don't want to be working at the KFC
so you can pay her child support, do you?

How many of you are in this situation?

A lot of you. A lot of you are baby fathers.

SHAME ON YOU.

You know what? Most of us don't deserve the
company of women.

But for some reason, many women seem to like
having us around.

I for one, am mystified. These highly intelligent,
beautiful, funny and wonderful AND A MILLION
TIMES BETTER THAN US females actually put up
with us. And put up with our SHIT. And it is SHIT,
guys, and you KNOW it's SHIT. Sometimes, you're

thinking, "I can't believe I just got away with that."
Aren't you? Aren't You?

But you know what? You don't get away with it.
Because every time you hurt a female, something
inside you, the best part of you dies. I want you to
say something to yourselves, I want you to say;

I will NEVER again hurt the woman in my life. I am
grateful to the woman in my life for being in my
life.

Because Women are goddesses
Women are angels.
I worship the woman in my life.

He turns on bended knee.

Oh yes I do.

scene twenty

MINKLE/ JERRY

JERRY   He used to tie me to the pear tree when... I had my
period. Usually just four or five hours.... One time
he left me there all night. It was August, so all night,
I watched these pears, falling down around me,
splatting onto the ground. The squirrels pick them
and eat half of them and then they drop them and
the bees finish them off. So I'm tied to the tree in the
pitch black, well, not quite pitch because the light
from the streetlight next street over is sort of shining
on part of my face, but it's the standing up, it's the
standing up all night, I hadda pee my pants twice,
it's hot, it's cold, I'm stinking, blood running down
my legs I bleed heavily, heavily on my periods my
legs are crumpling my poor dog Daisy she used to
bark all night from inside. He untied me in the
morning. With an erection. I didn't scream because
I didn't want to upset the neighbours, Sam and
Charlie, they were such nice guys, they brought me
peaches and apples from the family orchard in
Niagara, I made jam for them. I didn't want them

to think I was such a dork I would go and get
myself tied to a pear tree, besides, I would really
bleed on my periods, I mean a bleeding like I would
go through a tampon every twenty minutes and
well, I was embarrassed. He untied me when he
came down to let the cats in at six. He would
whisper in my ear and then lead me in and... use
me like an inflatable doll for hours, then he went to
work. I wouldn't talk to him for a few days, but
then, it was like it never happened, and things
would go back to normal. And I would almost
forget he even DID it, like it was a dream, like you
do with a very bad dream.

And you want to know why I stayed with him?
Why? Because basically, because I did-not-want-to
be alone. I was very very afraid of being alone. Isn't
that pathetic? Isn't that just so pathetic?

scene twenty-one

Phone rings.

DELPHINE   Hello? Hello? Hello? Hello? Hello Hello Hello? Why
do you keep calling me? Is there something wrong
with your head? Are you trying to TERRIFY me
or INTIMIDATE me? Well you are NOT doing
anything of the KIND, I am a DOCTOR, I have seen
everything, I am hardly going to be FRIGHTENED
by the likes of YOU, I am merely IRRITATED,
alright? So I would like you to stop irritating me—

JERRY   Dr. Moth this is your biological daughter.

DELPHINE hangs up. Tries to catch her breath.
SFX: The phone rings again. DELPHINE answers.
Beat.

DELPHINE   Do... please continue.

JERRY   My name is Geraldine Lee? I uh... tracked down
your number through Hamilton Children Services
And uh... I just... I hope you don't mind... I just
really wanted, to say "hello."

DELPHINE	*(long silence)* Well dear, I had really rather closed that chapter of my life.
JERRY	Oh I know, I know, I fully understand, and yeah, I don't want ANYTHING, I just really wanted to... say hello...
DELPHINE	Well. Hello, then. Hullo.
JERRY	And... oh, well, in case I have a child, I wanted to... ask you if there was any medical—
DELPHINE	No. No there is nothing... medical, as a physician, I would have alerted the agency, if anything had...
JERRY	Oh, oh, of course, I'm sorry, I just thought it prudent to...
DELPHINE	...Have you um... called before?
JERRY	Oh, um, yah, a few times.
DELPHINE	How many times.
JERRY	Oh, well, quite a few.
DELPHINE	And did you send me a... poem?
JERRY	Yeah.
DELPHINE	Aha.
JERRY	Sorry. I am so sorry. I should never have... intruded on your life like that, I wanted to speak I wanted so much to say something.
DELPHINE	Why didn't you? Why did you let me babble on like a...
JERRY	I don't know... I loved hearing your voice.
DELPHINE	Well. You have frightened me. You have caused me sleepless nights. I hope you are happy.
JERRY	I'm sorry, I'm very sorry—I didn't mean to—
DELPHINE	This is all very messy and chaotic and not the way I like to do things.

JERRY   Did you never ever suspect that the caller—

DELPHINE   No! I thought you were a rude boy...

JERRY   I'm sorry. I hope you can... forgive me.

DELPHINE   ...I... have always been curious about you...

JERRY   Thank you. Do I—sound the way you imagined?

DELPHINE   No.

JERRY   In what way?

DELPHINE   I can't say.

JERRY   You are exactly what I imagined.

DELPHINE   Oh my.

JERRY   Listen, do you think there is any possibility of me coming for a short visit?

DELPHINE   —This is very hard for me to say, and hate hate to appear blunt, but I am truly not able to ever see you, dear, as much as I would like to it just will not be possible. Ever. I'm sorry.

JERRY   Oh. You... want your privacy.

DELPHINE   Oh bless your heart I am very happy that you have had a nice life, I have wished that for you many times.

JERRY   You have?

DELPHINE   Oh yes dear, Oh yes I have.

JERRY   I could feel it.

DELPHINE   Well... that's nice, dear, and I am glad to have this conversation with you but this... truly will have to be the last. The last and the final. That is just... the way things are. There are... many... reasons. Can you... try to... understand that?

JERRY   Sure. Sure, it must be very weird for you.

l to r: Nancy Palk, Randi Helmers
photo by Nir Baraket

DELPHINE Who gave you my telephone number?

JERRY The person there, she said it was my—right.

DELPHINE Oh my goodness, what about my.... Rights? Do I not have rights then?

JERRY I'm sorry.

DELPHINE Listen. I have a very, VERY busy medical practice, Do you understand? When I go in tomorrow I see little Brendan Donnelly first, he has had the croup for three weeks—

JERRY Can I... at least... call you once in a while?

DELPHINE And a young mother dying of pancreatic cancer at this very moment in the hospital, and two patients passing kidney stones and aunts and nephews and sisters of course Mrs. Smale awaiting her dreadful results, Oh no. No I don't think so. For reasons you will never know but must accept, my darling daughter, I think that this one conversation... will be our last.

JERRY   But what would be the harm in occasional...

DELPHINE   Oh well, I—must.... Absolutely forbid you to
               contact me again my dear.

JERRY   No. You can't forbid me. You are ethically obliged.

DELPHINE   It was only an accident of biology that connects us
               at all, dear, no offense intended none at all you
               sound perfectly sweet but you must not contact me
               ever again, in any way at all. Do you understand?
               I am afraid that is firm and final. And you must
               accept it and move on, just move right along, dear.

JERRY   But I...

DELPHINE   Firm and is final. *(She hangs up.)* Firm and is final.

               DELPHINE is devatated.

ACT TWO

scene one

Fourteen years earlier.

JERRY   Professor Dodger?

DODGE   Uh huh. Just a second. Hi! Come on in, sit down, if you can find a spot. How can I help you Ms. umm—oh I am sorry, I can't remember your name, with over 100 students in the one class.

JERRY   Oh, call me Jerry, please. Geraldine JOY Lee?

DODGE   So. What brings you here, Geraldine? Do you mind if I eat my lunch? I have only twenty minutes before teaching 120 students again! It's avocado, wonderfully nourishing and—

JERRY   —disturbing.

DODGE   I beg your pardon?

JERRY   What you said I found it… disturbing.

DODGE   Okay. Fair enough. What part of it, Jerry.

JERRY   About the devil,

DODGE   Uh Huh.

JERRY   Inside us.

DODGE   Uh huh..

JERRY   I am religious. I come from a very Christian family and I have been taught to believe that the devil is OUTSIDE of us I mean, I KNOW he is outside of us and…. He… he makes his way in, like a tape worm, gets inside us and deprives us of our nutrients, our mortality until we are starving, spiritually starving to death.

DODGE   YAH! Okay! That is delightful to me that you have been thinking so very seriously about this!!!

            But some people believe… the devil is not only inside us but IS us. Whaddya think of them apples?

JERRY	No! No! That is just WRONG and you are very wrong to teach this... heresy, apostasy; The students trust in you, and...
DODGE	"Beware of false prophets, which come to you in sheep's clothing, but inwardly, they are ravening wolves."
JERRY	Matthew 7.
DODGE	Is that what you think about me?
JERRY	No. Yes. I mean, I'm just not sure. That's why I came to see you.
DODGE	Some people think that we have the seed of evil inside us, and all we need to do is to water that seed, and it will grow. Like a thicket.
JERRY	WAIT. I have been brought up to... to... see the devil as... as an outsider. Trying to make his way in. And I don't think you should be...
DODGE	An... invader.
JERRY	Like... like an illegal alien. Like—
DODGE	An immigrant?
JERRY	In a way... well no, I mean only if that person were trying to do harm.... My mom used to put little love notes in my backpack, I would open my snack, which were always homemade coconut cream buns and there would be a pink post-it note and it would say "Mommy loves you and Daddy loves you and most of all, God loves you." And... I don't believe that a God who loves me would allow... a devil... to.... If God loves me, I do not have the devil inside me. Not even a little. I am clean inside. My soul is clean I have never even been TEMPTED by the devil.
DODGE	*(now suspicious of her, is silent)* Do you ever have unkind thoughts?
JERRY	No.

DODGE   You are lying to yourself, Geraldine.

JERRY   No. I love everyone, I have been taught to to to to...

DODGE   Never a lie?

JERRY   NO.

DODGE   Not even a "white lie".

JERRY   No.

DODGE   How much are you doing for the children who die every day?

JERRY   I am praying for them, sir.

DODGE   And is it working?

JERRY   I like to think...

DODGE   It is not working Jerry, you have to actually DO something. Jerry. You are benefiting from their suffering.

JERRY   I am NOT benefiting, how can you SAY that?

DODGE   Think about it, Ms. Lee.

JERRY   Ahhhh. Listen. I did not come in here to be scolded by you I came in here to tell you that I was offended, on behalf of myself, and Our Lord God by the way you have been talking and I would like you to meet with my pastor or or listen why don't we just kneel down and pray right now...   ·

         (*She takes his hand.*) "Dear Lord God in Heaven, Lord we just ask you into our hearts holy holy"— Do you have faith in the LORD?

DODGE   Sometimes.

JERRY   But you have moments of doubt?

DODGE   Of course.

JERRY   And in those moments of doubt, is that when you see the devil?

DODGE   No.

JERRY   When?

DODGE   I don't know.

JERRY   When you look at me?

            Moment.

DODGE   I'm sorry.

JERRY   Sir? It's just… I have this nightmare, um, quite
            frequently, actually that I am in a room—a room,
            beyond the room, I mean, nobody can see it has
            no window, no way in and no way out and I never
            ever will get out and… and then I notice a small
            shadow there, and I realize that that it is the devil
            in there with me in this small, suffocating room
            with no window or door, and a too bright buzzing
            light, a evil I can't see but I can feel, like a stomach
            ache, and he is—

            JERRY moves closer towards DODGE.

            ### scene two

DELPHINE   Well you silly woman you KNEW she would find
            you one day, didn't you? You knew she would find
            you and corner you and make you feel GUILT. But
            you didn't know the GUILT would come in the
            form of a gas. Good LORD what a punishment
            I can't go five minutes without having to let a huge
            ripping fart go; the motility of my intestinal tract is
            impaired—the street of YOU calling me, my dear
            daughterine has CRIMPED my intestines and so old
            food just sits there and the acid transforms it to gas
            and the smell is so appalling I can't even lie in my
            own bed. I can't actually leave the house until the
            motility has returned you dreadful girl. You
            dreadful and awful and dreadful girl you have
            given me guilt gas.

scene three

JERRY and AZIZ dancing.

AZIZ   *Inteh-hull-weh ("You are beautiful" in Arabic.)*
...MACHALLAH!

JERRY   What did you say?

AZIZ   You know what I said.

JERRY   You said, I am beautiful.

AZIZ   How did you know that?

JERRY   Because. Of the way you said it. Because. Nobody has ever said that to me before.

AZIZ   You are beautiful inside. I don't care about the outside. That is Western Corruption, Illusion. You have a pure and beautiful soul.

JERRY   Thank you.

AZIZ   You are welcome. Am I welcome, Jerry Joy?

JERRY   You are welcome. You have been welcome.

AZIZ   I will have been welcome. We will have been dancing for—

JERRY   We will have been holding hands for—

AZIZ   We will have been looking into one another's eyes for—
"What Allah said to the Rose
And caused it to laugh in full blown beauty,
He said to my heart
And made it a hundred times more beautiful."

They dance for a while.

AZIZ   You are my home, my home is in your soul.

JERRY   Really? Does that mean we are... living together?

AZIZ   We are living together. In my soul.

JERRY	And you're cooking for me?
AZIZ	I will never cook.
JERRY	OH if you live with me, you are cooking.
AZIZ	Never. I will never cook for a woman.
JERRY	You don't mean that.
AZIZ	Yes. I do. A man in my country does not cook or clean. But might have to cook because I have tasted your cooking.
JERRY	Will you kiss me?
AZIZ	No. I cannot kiss you.
JERRY	Uh oh. Do I have bad breath? Minkle says I have really bad breath sometimes, I have a Fisherman's Friend in my purse.
AZIZ	I cannot kiss you.
JERRY	Oh. I'm sorry. Because of your… faith.
AZIZ	You understand.
JERRY	Oh yes, I understand faith. I had… a lot of faith at one time.
AZIZ	You do not have it now?
JERRY	I don't know.
AZIZ	Look at the sun. Do you see the power of the sun? That is the power of faith. Faith is the most powerful energy there is, it can…
JERRY	Move mountains?
AZIZ	Yes!
JERRY	But there are some things it can't do.
AZIZ	It cannot change what is meant to be.
JERRY	You know what I have faith in? I have faith in you. In you. *(He holds her.)* Tighter.

AZIZ	Yes.
JERRY	TIGHTER.
AZIZ	I am afraid I will crush you.
JERRY	You could never crush me. I love you.
AZIZ	What?
JERRY	I love you. I LUFF YOU. I LOVE LOVE I am MAD CRAZY WILD…
AZIZ	I love. What does this mean?
JERRY	Like A LOT. CHERISH. RESPECT, would DIE for…
AZIZ	I would die for you.
JERRY	You would? You would really?
AZIZ	Without question.
JERRY	I love love love love love love…
AZIZ	Stop behaving in this manner. Women in my country do not speak like this.
JERRY	Like what?
AZIZ	Like a child. Why do you speak like this? Why?
JERRY	Because. Because I am so happy, that I feel free, free at last because I love you so much that I feel somehow, safe, that I could… climb inside you. Can I climb inside you? And then look out your eyes? Then nobody could hurt me. And I wouldn't be afraid.
AZIZ	Geraldine, where is your faith? Why are you afraid? Do you not know that the time of your death is fixed from the moment you are born, and nothing, nothing you do can change that? Remember, there is nothing to fear.

l to r: Tom McCamus, Randi Helmers, Chick Reid
photo by Nir Baraket

scene four

MINKLE and JERRY in classroom, working on large body traces of the kids.

JERRY   You'll never guess what, I talked to the mother.

MINKLE   No way. You actually spoke?

JERRY   She told me to get lost.

MINKLE   Sounds fair to me.

JERRY   I guess.

MINKLE   Oh, look at his sweet little head. No, really, you okay with it?

JERRY   Fine. She has a right to a life.

MINKLE   She does have a right to a life. She totally does. So what'd she sound like?

JERRY   Like I always knew she would sound. Like a voice that has always been inside my ear.

MINKLE   So. You aren't gonna call her anymore, right?

JERRY	Why would I? I heard her voice, She heard mine, that's all I need. Anyway, I have Aziz. All my love is flowing to him. Oceans of love. It's unbelievable.
MINKLE	Look at Shareefa. Such an angel. What the hell can I say about winter? "Winter is a time for..."
JERRY	Freezing.
MINKLE	Yeah. That'll do. But do you ever think, like just for an uneasy minute, that he's makin up the whole refugee thing? And he's like a hustler from Lahore who wants the good life, the widescreen TV and the jumbo shrimp and the sweet pussy with a steady job?

A mosque, AZIZ prays, on a small, beautiful oriental carpet.

AZIZ	We are higher than heaven, more noble than the angels. Why not go beyond them? Our goal is the Supreme Majesty. What has the fine pearl to do with the world of dust—?

scene five

MINKLE	So how was it going on the Tilt-a-Whirl after seven years sitting out? Was it good? Bad? Passionate? Perfunctory? A lot of foreign guys are actually quite perfunctory, in my own experience.
JERRY	Minkle, you know I'm not really comfortable talking about...
MINKLE	Did ya have that exploding grapefruit in your head you used to tell me about? I always envied you that, shit, I've never had more than a raisin.

Well, maybe a plum. With Francis, it's a plum. And that's why I'm his love slave till they toss me on the ventilator.

Beat.

So we haven't heard from Lucifer in a while. Do you think maybe he's calmed down? Or found himself a table dancer with a pierced tongue?

JERRY	I'm so happy with Aziz it's like it was all a bad dream.
MINKLE	We shouldn't get too comfortable, though, you know? Sometimes those "bad dreams" have a way of...
JERRY	Look. At the light coming through that window.
MINKLE	It's the archangel Gabriel. Come to annunciate me!

A bell rings. They look out the window at the kids at recess.

Oh. Here they come. And I have a major birthday party exclusion disaster going on.

JERRY	Minkle.
MINKLE	Right here.
JERRY	This may be hard for you to understand, but what you were talking about? Is never going to happen with us. It's way, way beyond that.
MINKLE	Of course. Like Heloise and Abelard. You're the nun, he's the monk. No stains on the sheets. It's sensible.

scene six

DODGE teaches.

DODGE	What happens when we commit an act of violence? When we commit an act of violence, we lose our human shape, don't we? We TRANSMOGRIFY. Yes, we become monsters. Every person in this world has become a monster at one time or another, you aren't the only ones. Listen: Each of you is a monster movie, you know that movie about the kid who becomes a wolfman that's what all of you did! Your hands grew gigantic and your muscles burst out of your skin and your snout grew and your eyes became red and you grew teeth and claws and became wolfmonsters. *(howls)*

It's a rush unlike any other, isn't it guys? Like doin 180 on the highway, but you know, you KNOW, you're going to crash and you keep going faster.

So how do you stop it? How do you stop this transmogrification? You poor guys, you are nothing but pawns; your violence is so over-determined you didn't have a chance it's a goddamned thicket grown over thousands of years of history and it's almost impossible to clear you have to be SUPERMAN to clear a thicket like that, my friends. How many of you have the strength to be Superman?

scene seven

JERRY and AZIZ

JERRY	You're mad at me today.
AZIZ	No.
JERRY	Did somebody hurt you? Try to rob your cab? I heard some teenaged girls stabbed a driver today that wasn't—
AZIZ	Please. Do not touch me.
JERRY	Oooohkay.
AZIZ	Respect my faith.
JERRY	Please, Aziz, don't be angry with me.
AZIZ	I am not angry with you.
JERRY	I feel like you are. Please, tell me, what is inside you?
AZIZ	What do you think?
JERRY	I would never say.
AZIZ	You say too much. And you ask too much. You are inquisitive.

JERRY   Inquisitive? I haven't even asked you where you are
          from! Or ANYTHING about your life before this,
          how can you...?

AZIZ   I am tired. Please. I would like true tea I need true
          tea. But here there is only Red Rose.

JERRY   I want so much to see you happy, but there is such
          a sadness—

AZIZ   That is in your eyes too, Geraldine.

                    Beat.

JERRY   And that's why we understand each other.

AZIZ   You... can never understand.

JERRY   I want to, Aziz.

AZIZ   My life is not here.

JERRY   Yes it IS, it IS here, with me and Sharzia.

AZIZ   This—is an amphetamine dreams, this life of
          outspoken supermarkets with too much bright
          coloured food from the dreams of starving children
          and and tin can movie actors red paint on their lips
          and sexuality as a serpent and laughing teenager
          boys who do not have to carry guns and kill people
          only drink alcohol and vomit in my cab this is a
          dream, I must leave this dream and I must wake up.

JERRY   Why do you say that?

                    Beat.

AZIZ   What is your favoured time of day?

JERRY   Evening. The light.

AZIZ   You always say "Ah yes, I so love the evening light,
          the smell of cooking food coming from houses, the
          people hurrying home with grocery bags, children
          coming home from lessons, playing hockey in the
          road," a falling of day, a rising of night. Imagine in
          my country the same, a time of day the heart is

strong the sun low spilling over the earth warm air,
women chatter, laugh, scold, making food over the
fires the smell a glory, my seven children, yes seven,
running here and there, my oldest daughters are
bathing the smaller ones, they are so clean, happy,
I am hungry, I want to eat, but my Sharzia, she
reminds me we must climb the tree to find the
highest bark for the healer has told us this bark has
special properties, it will help my mother-in-law
who has trouble to walk, I say "Come, we will climb
in the ash tree, together." It is not easy, my Uncle, he
helps us and Sharzia and I, we were high in the ash
tree we are scraping the… the bark of the ash tree it
is… a smell to intoxicate it is… and suddenly, the
sky moves down down and deep dark with
a sound like the groan before death of an animal as
if we are dreaming a most terrible dream: What we
have heard of but we have not imagined blackened
sky swings this way and this way dogs barking like
never/ engines/ trucks/ crowded with soldiers,
from nowhere, crash, yelling like soccer fans
running, with guns, with knives, blood, drunk,
vomiting, bottles, broken, obscenities, laughing,
our women, nervous, offering food, backing away,
grabbed, thrown, then screaming, the children,
running, in circles, "Mama, Mama," most of our
men away, at war, old men, 13-year-old boys,
fighting with their hands, children running,
bleeding, —seven year old Sashira holding my
little Jabal running running my wife, Esmira,
screaming at them to "Run, run never stop
running" holding the babies; fire, dog's fury,
kill on soldier, shot to death on ground too much
a swarming cannot see so much noise, so much
wind, so much shooting, tanks, shooting, gasoline,
and fire fire and thick black smoke.

You are wondering why I stayed in the tree?

JERRY   No. I know why.

AZIZ   Some of them, some of the bodies seemed to come
             to life while burning. When I returned to bury, I lift
             them, so blackened, so… burned… their skin… like
             a wrapping.

This is why I never sleep. How can I sleep until
I have done what I must do?

scene eight

JERRY and MINKLE.

JERRY   He's falling away from me.

MINKLE   They do that.

JERRY   I think he's leaving the country. Soon. After he told
          me about what happened, he said that he will never
          rest "Until I do what I must do."

MINKLE   Uh huh.

JERRY   What do you think he meant by that?

MINKLE   What do *you* think he meant by that?

JERRY   I think he meant—justice. Find the murderers and
          bring them to justice. It could take a very long time.

MINKLE   Or the time it takes to poach an egg. He straps on
          the dynamite.

JERRY   What are you suggesting? Oh Minkle, you are NOT
          assuming he is one of those…

MINKLE   This is the real world, Jerry. Read the papers.

JERRY   That is ridiculous. A ridiculous stupid racial
          stereotype and you ought to be ashamed of
          yourself.

MINKLE   I don't know. In my experience, justice doesn't
          usually happen. If I were him I'd want revenge.

JERRY   He is a loving father. He is the gentlest, kindest,
          most rational…

MINKLE   Jerry. Tell me. Tell me you wouldn't want revenge.

JERRY   I would NOT want revenge. I don't even know
          what that feels like. And neither does he. He wants

REDRESS, redemption NEVER revenge. I KNOW he would never ever hurt an innocent.

MINKLE   Okay okay okay okay. But the upshot is: the only man who ever loved you the way you should be loved...

JERRY   ...is leaving me.

MINKLE   I know. I know what it's like.

scene nine

JERRY conducts the children. She plays all the parts.

GIRL   I can't pay the rent.

EVIL MAN   You MUST pay the rent.

GIRL   I can't pay the rent.

EVIL MAN   You must pay the rent.

GIRL   I can't pay the rent.

EVIL MAN   You MUST pay the rent.

NICE MAN
HERO   I'LL pay the rent.

GIRL   MY HERO.

JERRY applauds the children.

JERRY   You guys are great that was FANtastic.

She senses DODGE.

Ahh. Hi... is there... something I can help you with? *(beat)* Yes, you're here to teach the Indonesian shadow puppets? That's the grades 3, 4, and 5. I think they're waiting for you in the gym. That's just down the stairs to the left.

She turns to the kids.

The puppet man is just leaving. He is going to show the bigger kids how to make puppets with SHADOWS. Have any of you ever…

He is still there.

Goodbye. *(beat)* I'm sorry. Goodbye. *(She looks to the children.)* "If you're happy and ya know it clap your hands… *(He claps.)* If you're happy and you know clap your hands… if you're happy and you know it and ya really want to show it, if you're happy and you know it clap your hands.

DODGE   See you tonight, angel! *(He disappears.)*

scene ten

MINKLE with SHARZIA

MINKLE   Hello there Sharzee what's shaking? You got a substitute today, huh? Do ya like her? Oh I know, nobody is as nice as Miss Jerry. She's got a big old headache that's what she told me. *(beat)* They did? Now why would they go and do that? Oh they did, did they. And who was the leader? Uh huh. No doubt she was. Well I don't like that one little bit. You know what? They will not bother you ever again I can promise you that. What am I gonna do to em? I'm gonna make em lick frozen metal fences and then ALL their tongues'll be stuck and… no, no of course not, I'll just talk to em. Give em detentions. *(beat)* Howz your dad doin'? Yah? He took you in the taxi? You lucky duck. *(beat)* You're moving? To your cousins in Kitchener? I see. Well. How long you going for, Sharz. A long long long time? Is that what your dad told ya? Uh huh. Well don't worry, biscuit, time just goes so fast you won't believe it. Yeah. Oh I know what that's like, when they make you eat yucky food, I used to hide mine in my shoes. Oh sweetie, don't be sad. I'm sure your dad will come back in a while. Lots of dads go away on business, love. Oh yes, he will, he will my love. And until he does, you can just talk to him in your dreams. I do that, with my mum and

dad, all the time. Yeah. And you know what else?
You can draw him pictures, one for every day.

scene eleven

AZIZ with SHARZIA.

AZIZ   And so the funny creature man tries the green eggs
and yes, yes he likes them, just the way you didn't
want to try Kraft dinner at your friend's house but
then you tried it and now you ask Baba to make it
every night. Terrible stuff.

He sings an Arabic lullaby.

*"NA MEE YA BINTI NA ME HABIBTI NA MEE YA
BINTI NA MEE…"*

AZIZ slowly backs out of the room.

scene twelve

JERRY's place, or classroom.

DODGE   I hope you don't mind, I climbed in the window.
Courtly love and all that. It's like whitewater
running through my veins, you know? Seeing you?
You don't want me to go away. You want me to stay.
Now that your boyfriend has left the country;
dumped you. What do you wanna bet he got the
call and he's going to go and blow himself up.
You'll see it on the news any day Jerry. You'll see he
is NOT the SAINT you think he is.

He's a ruthless bastard. Just like me. NO better than
me.

I'm sorry that he hurt you, Jerr. I myself would do
anything to make you happy. Anything in this
whole wide world. You know that, right? Because
you and I, we go way back. Thousands of years,
actually.

I am the only one who understands you, Jerr, no one else in the world will ever love you like I do. LOVE LOVE LOVE you every cell of your body every sign every word from your mouth every glance of your eyes every dance of your hands the way your hair falls over your naked shoulder we will burn.

scene thirteen

DELPHINE   Just because you gave birth to her does NOT mean you have ANY obligation to see her, do NOT feel guilty you behaved with PERFECT GRACIOUSNESS stop it! And don't think that yearning to see her is anything other than guilt, its certainly not some kind of primal mother... pang... no; no no no no don't think for a minute that you're going to tell her you're dying of Cancer to get yourself a long lost loving daughter to smear Vaseline on your lips when they are cracked to change the bedpan... to sit by the bed through the night as you struggle to breathe; you will not let her into your life because... because... you are afraid. Afraid as hell to die alone, with only an overworked nurse checking in now and then, or a palliative care volunteer with bad breath afraid that the rust has spread to the brain is rusting my brain—afraid that the fact I forgot my own name yesterday and couldn't remember my phone number means that I have weeks only weeks left to live. Afraid because I know that I will never—

She falls into his arms.

scene fourteen

DODGE teaches:

DODGE   YOU! How do you know you are alive? How do you know you are conscious? Beyond seeing hearing feeling tasting? Huh? How do you—yes, YOU there with the headphones TAKE OFF THE STINKING HEADPHONES, JEREMY, how do you know you are a YOU. And not HIM? You find that funny? Oh yes it's quite funny, it's hilarious to me that you think you have ANY identity apart from the guy next to you. Or him. Or me. Aren't we just all part of the same drippy batter?

What? You think you have an identity? Well okay, then,

What forms this identity? The smell of your farts?

Your hair, your jeans, the way you chew gum, the way you swear, you laugh—

"I am everything I have ever said or done. And I am everything that has ever been said to me. I am everything that one human being has ever done to another. I have a historical consciousness."

   Beat.

We don't REALLY know we exist until somebody looks at us, right? And really truly sees us. If nobody sees us, how do we know we exist? We look for ourselves in others and when we finally see ourselves VRROOOM! that is what we sometimes call love.

scene fifteen

   DODGE and JERRY on the street.

DODGE   Hey. How are you?

JERRY   Awake. Now.

DODGE   Thy lips are like a thread of scarlet.

JERRY   Dodge, that was—

DODGE   Destiny. You, me—cream, coffee; it's mythical Biblical: "my love feedeth among the lilies."

JERRY   A terrible, terrible—

DODGE   Our bed is green.

JERRY   —fall.

DODGE   No. Hey. Don't say that please. Don't say that.

JERRY   Terrible. Never.

DODGE   Jerry, you do not mean that. Christ. It's the first time I have felt like a human being in in—

JERRY   That will never ever happen again Dodge. It was despair, it was.

DODGE   It was real, Jerry. God was there, between our bodies, I felt that YOU felt that.

JERRY   Please. Let me goooo.

DODGE grips her face and pushes her away.

scene sixteen

MINKLE   As soon as we can get our shit together, Jerr we're outta here.

JERRY   Sharzia.

MINKLE   Sharzia is going to be just fine with her cousins; in a couple of weeks you'll be nothing more than a distant memory, that's what kids are like, they're bouncy.

JERRY   He's going to get me. Soon.

MINKLE   Stop talking, start packing, honey come nightfall we're driving until alls we smell is sea salt and early bird dinners.

scene seventeen

MINKLE and DELPHINE in her office.

DELPHINE   Minkle Carletti?

MINKLE   Straight up? I don't have foot fungus. I'm a friend of your biological daughter. Here on a mission.

DELPHINE   Oh my God.

MINKLE   All I'm gonna ask you to do is be reasonable. My friend is going to die.

DELPHINE   I beg your pardon?

MINKLE   Jerry Joy Lee. Your biological daughter. And all she wants is a simple meeting.

DELPHINE   A simple meeting.

MINKLE   It could save her life. And even if it doesn't, it will help her die peacefully. To be frank… she has terminal cancer. Stage four. Liver. It's that cancer they say is like Quaker Oatmeal when you pour it outta the box, you breathe on it and it's all over the kitchen.

DELPHINE   Well. How is she…

MINKLE   How do you think? It's basically over. And all she wants is one meeting with you. That's all she asks she wants nothing else.

           Silence.

DELPHINE   You know, I have to say, I don't believe you.

MINKLE   WHAT?

DELPHINE   I can always tell when someone is lying. A kind of crinkle in the voice.

MINKLE   Alright. You got me, I was lying.

DELPHINE   She will just have to accept that our lives are not ever going to—

MINKLE   What if I told you the truth?

DELPHINE   And that is?

MINKLE   That her ex-husband is going to kill her any day. Any HOUR. It is the truth. And there's no stopping him. I tried to hire some Mafia guys in Las Vegas, some Satan's Choice around here, no one will get involved. They don't fucking care.

DELPHINE   Well. Yes. I know the situation and I—I have had
            several patients I have directed to women's shelters.

MINKLE   Don't make me LARF. If someone wants to find you
            you cannot hide, get it? GET IT? This is a done deal,
            baby, a Greek tragedy it was fixed from the first day
            they met, the gods were pissing themselves.

            Listen, you cunt, if you don't see her I will go to the
            press with this, about your cold and ruthless
            behaviour, all your patients will know about it...

DELPHINE   Is she really in—serious—

MINKLE   You will go to heaven if you do this for her. And
            hell if you don't. In fact, I will kiss you if you don't,
            so we will both go. To hell. Together. You will never
            be rid of me.

DELPHINE   Oh. Well. Of course. Of course, I will see her. Yes.
            But please understand. It can only be ONE meeting.

MINKLE   Honey. There's only time for one meeting. Now
            listen: my pee is about the colour of jasmine tea.
            Is that normal?

scene eighteen

DODGE teaches.

DODGE   Human emotions are something else, aren't they?
            Stronger than heroin speed ecstasy FAR stronger
            than any drug in the universe. We are—like
            playdoh, like dogshit—we lose all our will we are
            almost HELPLESS when in the hold of an emotion.

            Most of you are helpless right now, in the thrall of
            some emotion: SEX, GREED, HATRED, FEAR the
            four Gods of Man.

            It's not just you. Oh no. I myself have been there.
            Oh Yes. I have. I am. I am. In the thrall of... of...
            I can't even name it but it's like... the real me, the
            person that I know I am is is getting smaller and
            smaller, this tiny mosquito in the corner while the

other. The other is growing like a Manitoba maple tree. Listen; listen guys please listen to me. When you feel the thing, the choking weed growing inside of you, destroy it; vaporize it with pure clean water your power of reason. Open the door. I beg you. Breathe in the air. Go for a walk, a run, a bike ride. But DON'T give in to your rage. Please. NEVER give in to your rage. The penitentiaries are full of people who gave in to rage. HELL is full of people who gave into rage.

Open the door.

DELPHINE & DODGE Breathe in the air.

scene nineteen

MINKLE and JERRY in a car.

MINKLE Get outta here. We're fine, I have my radio and my cell, me and Francis are having a fight about money and sex, the dog's havin a snooze, we're good. Now go, and have a really swell time with the old doll.

JERRY approaches DELPHINE in the dark.

JERRY Hello, Hello?

DELPHINE Hello

JERRY Dr. Delphine... Moth?

DELPHINE *(turns on flashlight)* Are you Geraldine, then?

JERRY Yeah. Hi. Hi. Oh. God. Thank you so much for coming.

DELPHINE I can't stay long.

JERRY Oh. Of course, I know you are very busy. This, it really means a lot to me that you came.

DELPHINE I've brought a flashlight for you too.

JERRY Oh. Thanks.

DELPHINE   It's very dark here.

JERRY   Wow. You are way more beautiful than I imagined. I mean…

DELPHINE   Well thank you I do think you flatter me, dear.

JERRY   No, really. Do I… look different than the way you imagined?

DELPHINE   I didn't imagine…

JERRY   Well. It's a lovely night.

DELPHINE   I find it chilly. But then I'm always cold, ever since the menopause, always cold except for the hot flashes, which are like a little roller coaster ride, actually, I quite enjoy them, a kind of theatre of the body. So you see I have agreed to come and meet you because your little friend Minkle came to visit me.

JERRY   Thank you.

DELPHINE   I really am very sorry. If what she said is true. Is it—

JERRY   Yeah.

DELPHINE   Aha.

JERRY   Well. Thanks for…

DELPHINE   I would not be human if I did not respond in some way. I have a list of names and telephone numbers that I give to all my patients who—find themselves in this circumstance.

JERRY   Oh! Great.

DELPHINE   These organizations have been a tremendous help.

JERRY   Sure.

DELPHINE   I've brought some hot chocolate for us. *(She opens the thermos and pours.)*

JERRY   Oh, thank you, I love hot chocolate. *(They drink.)*

DELPHINE   But I hope you can understand that I cannot bring you, fold you into my life like egg yolks into sugar, it just would not be possible.

JERRY   Oh, I know what, I don't expect that. I just… I really wanted to meet you. And I feel better already.

DELPHINE   Good. I am very glad.

   Beat.

JERRY   Why did you want to meet here? In this dark creepy part—it's like a ghost park.

DELPHINE   It… was… a fairground… as a child, I would ride with my sisters on that Ferris Wheel.

   Beat.

JERRY   Can you… listen, I vow to never bother you again, really, I just… I am just so curious about the circumstances around my…

DELPHINE   Yes. I thought you might ask about that… it's so long ago now I… well it's not something I like to think about, Jerry, because it was… it was really not…. It was one of those… I grew up in a very strict Catholic family, you understand, on the east coast in a very small town I was very sheltered I didn't know what an erection was until I was sixteen; truly, imagine me, Delphine Moth, fourteen years old, I hadn't ever HAD a period, I was a really late bloomer, I had about two days of pains, so I though I was finally going to menstruate like my friends, but then I was in geography class giving a little talk on volcanoes, I remember exactly what I was saying, I was saying, on "The Island of Krakatoa, the volcano erupted in 1867 killing 36,000 souls" And suddenly I felt this terrific pain and I said, "Excuse me I am not feeling well at all if you don't mind may I be excused Sister Barney?" That was her name. And so I ran down the hallway to the washroom and I went into the stall and then the pain well I'm sure you've heard what labour is like. I felt I became a Krakatoa I felt like I was a mountain in a very cold a freezing country a tall

pink and red mountain and I thought I heard drums
and the drums were drumming louder and louder
and the people the women were singing the air was
darkening the pressure in my head the pain the
pure horror of pain. I couldn't scream, the janitor
Bill would hear me. I bit on my arm and it was as
if the volcano exploded and the people ran ran
in their bare feet the hot hot lava catching them,
drowning them, she was drowning in the lava
she had to get away from the lava, she she pulled
herself away, looked into the white round pool
and there was a bloody creamy the lava had killed
a child she bit she bit off the vine that had strangled
the child she picked up the child she would save the
child she she heard a mewling a crying run run
away they are coming after the baby they want to
sacrifice the baby running down the hall "Miss
Moth, Miss Moth may I ask where you might be?"
Catch the bus goes way out only two of us on the
bus blood running down my legs feeling dizzy very
dizzy okay, Come and Stay A While campground
run down the long long driveway, past the few
trailers to the fairground, my blood running down
my legs all over the ground saw the Ferris Wheel
rusting.

Ferris wheel and I saved the baby I put her on the
Ferris wheel away from harm from the hot hot lava
and "Krakatoa Girl" ran all the way back to the
school on the hot lava sliding sliding for a typing
test. Mother said, I had to do well in typing if
I wanted to be a doctor. Mr. Hale the typing teacher
with the goatee and the white shoes, he noticed the
blood was dripping onto the floor below me. "Oh
no, that's just lava said I, I was just in a volcano
explosion you know, over the the island on the
island" All the kids were talking behind their
hands, and Sister Johnny she put her hands on my
shoulders and I blacked right out and I didn't come
to until I was in the hospital. In mental hospital
there was a horse in my room and a small volcano.

Beat.

My older cousin Shelley she sat there with me for weeks; she held my hand, she helped me breathe and said "Never never feel guilty; you did nothing wrong" I did nothing wrong. I did nothing wrong. I am not responsible for you.

I'm sorry.

JERRY Look. Just look at that moonlight coming through the branches.

DELPHINE Onliest Aloneliest.

JERRY &
DELPHINE The wind is with thee.

Beat.

DELPHINE I'm one of two doctors for 10,000 people.

JERRY I could help you.

DELPHINE Oh yes. I am sure you could. And you would. You are clearly a very kind person.

JERRY I think you need me to help you. I think you need me badly right now.

DELPHINE No.

JERRY Yes. I can see, behind your eyes.

DELPHINE No.

JERRY I know! Maybe, maybe in thirty years when you're dying maybe then, then you would let me just come in and hold your hand, and wipe your face with a warm towel?

DELPHINE *(laughs and laughs but the laughter becomes silent and thoughtful)* You need to take care of yourself right now my dear.

JERRY It matters to you? Does it matter to you?

DELPHINE Every life matters to me.

JERRY That's... cold.

DELPHINE   Maybe.

JERRY   It's... ruthless.

DELPHINE   Alright.

JERRY   —What about letting me call you on your birthday, and maybe you call me on mine.

DELPHINE   It's getting late.

JERRY   NO.

DELPHINE   I'm leaving now.

JERRY   NO.

DELPHINE   Whether or not you want me to leave is...

JERRY   Noooooo!

DELPHINE   What is this supposed to mean?

JERRY   Anger

DELPHINE   What?

JERRY   The volcano.

DELPHINE   That was hallucinatory, a momentary psychosis brought on by Catholic guilt, and and hemorrhage—

> *AZIZ and DODGE, in separate spotlights, appear standing.*

JERRY   *(in an explosion)* RAAAAAAAGE... RAAAAAAAGE... RAAAAAAAGE...

> *DELPHINE moves towards her, caresses her and calms her.*

(crying) Mother...

DELPHINE   Water...

JERRY   ...ash

DELPHINE   *(sings)* "Ring around the rosie…. A pocket full of posies"

Ashes ashes

JERRY   We all Fall

DELPHINE   Fall

>   *Beat. They are very close and full of love.*

Do not be afraid.

>   *DELPHINE retreats and JERRY is alone.*

scene twenty

>   *JERRY alone.*

JERRY   Okay. Here I am, in the dark. All alone. Aren't you going to come and get me? I know that you're out there. I know that you followed me here Dodge, come out and talk to me.

DODGE   *(a voice in the dark)* How are your parents?

JERRY   They died in a car accident. On their way to a Christmas party in Red Deer.

DODGE   Oh. My God, I'm so sorry, they were fantastic people; your mum was a GREAT cribbage player, wasn't she? Your dad and I would talk about the World Cup… remember when we all celebrated Chinese New Year and he made dim sum? Jerr, I just followed you because I… wanted to talk to you. I have done a lot of thinking and firstly I… would like to apologize for my… shameful behaviour towards you; I don't pretend to understand it but I will tell you that I have… conquered it and… secondly, that I would… like… to have you back in my life.

JERRY   Dodge. You know the answer to that.

>   *Enter AZIZ — as JERRY's dreams in full Muslim dress. DELPHINE, MINKLE and AZIZ are there, but are voices in her head. Beat.*

AZIZ	Geraldine. Look at the sun. Do you see the power of the sun? That is the power of faith. Faith is the most powerful energy there is.
DELPHINE	Like rolling thunder, clapping.
DODGE	I will have you back, one way or the other.
JERRY	This isn't rational, Dodge. I think you need medication, I'll take you to emergency right now.
DODGE	They will find us here, together, by the rusted Ferris wheel… the rough green lake. We will see each other's final moments Jerr, what could be more intimate than that?
MINKLE	When a tiger is cornered, Jerr, what does she do?
DODGE	Looking into each other's eyes, just like before. Remember how we used to stare into each other's eyes for hours and hours we wouldn't eat we wouldn't sleep.
DELPHINE	The wind is with thee.
JERRY	How Dodge? How do you propose to take, to end my life?
DODGE	I'm going to whisper in your ear? WHORE.
AZIZ	Inteh—hull—weh.
JERRY	*(beat)* Why?
DODGE	You know why.
DELPHINE	Krakatoa girl.
JERRY	You don't want to do this, Dodge, this is not you.
DODGE	Remember the time we were swimming out to the seals off of Wreck Beach and you were caught in the riptide and it swept you out to sea?
AZIZ	I would die for you, without question.
DODGE	Remember when you tried to swim against it and you almost drowned?

JERRY	Listen. I know that you are a strong man. A strong man and a GOOD man.
DODGE	I am a good man. I'm a goddamned SAINT.
JERRY	Then talk yourself out of it Dodge.
DODGE	What the fuck do you think I've been doing for the past three months, BITCH, and then you come along and treat me like a piece of dogshit and then I have to start AGAIN, and AGAIN, and a—
JERRY	What have you been doing, Dodge?
MINKLE	When a tiger is cornered, Jerr.
JERRY	Why me? I'm just a real ordinary gal.
DELPHINE	You did nothing wrong.
JERRY	I am your friend.
AZIZ	You have a pure and beautiful soul.
JERRY	And I love you as my friend.
DODGE	You LOVE the DEVIL?
JERRY	You are not the devil, there is no devil, there is you.
DODGE	You LIE, you LIE to me you SLUT, you fucking DEVIL.
DELPHINE	Do not be afraid.
DODGE	I'm drowning here Devilbitch.
MINKLE	Well, what does a cornered tiger do?
JERRY	Save yourself.
DODGE	I'm drowning and YOU—
MINKLE	Tear his fucking throat out or die trying.
JERRY	Save yourself, Dodge—
DODGE	—You don't fucking CARE, it's moving faster and faster.

DELPHINE   A small volcano.

DODGE   I can't even fucking SEE FUCK can't see—
a goddamn—

JERRY   —Can see, you can see,

MINKLE   We will do what we have to do.

DODGE   Can't see the… the…

DELPHINE   Daughter.

JERRY   God. Between us…

AZIZ   Until I do, what I must do.

JERRY   Come.

DODGE   Don't. Don't, Jerry, GO, please.

AZIZ   There is nothing to fear.

DELPHINE   Water

JERRY   Give me your hand.

DODGE   NO.

JERRY   Give me your hand. DO not be afraid.

> *She reaches for his hand. DODGE reaches out, she pulls him up. He bows to her, kisses her hand, and turns his back to the audience and walks away, as if disappearing.*
>
> *JERRY collapses with relief, and joy. The others converge on her. (except AZIZ, who watches or disappears) A kind of embrace, moment of joy.*

scene twenty-one

> *JERRY and MINKLE in car. MINKLE drives. JERRY sleeps. A horn. JERRY wakes, with a start.*

JERRY   Ahhhh. Where are we?

MINKLE	About six hours outside of Miami.
JERRY	You getting sleepy? Want me to drive?
MINKLE	Nah. You're a terrible driver, go back to sleep.
JERRY	Can't go back to sleep. Don't want to go back to the dream.
MINKLE	Oh, please don't tell me your dream.
JERRY	I dreamt I was dead. That he—that I wasn't able to talk him out of it... if it wasn't for you guys... that's what would have...
MINKLE	I wonder what that means, dreaming you're dead. I've never dreamt I was dead. Lots of falling off cliffs, being chased by guys with knives, being pushed, being strangled, attacked by killer snakes and dogs but never dead.

> *Beat.*

JERRY	...Minkle?
MINKLE	Uh huh.
JERRY	Is this...? Are we...?
MINKLE	March break, baby, we are gonna get our groove back, lie around the pool in tangerine bikinis, drink Cosmopolitans out of carved out pineapples, have sweet poetry whispered in our ears by fiendishly handsome Cuban-Americans—two old girls getting young again in Never Never land.
JERRY	WhoooooHooooo! Wow. Minkle. Look at the sun. Do you see the power of that sun?

> *MINKLE honks her horn.*

> *The end.*

Judith Thompson is the author of *The Crackwalker, White Biting Dog, I Am Yours, Lion in the Streets, Sled, Perfect Pie, Habitat, Capture Me, Enoch Arden* and *My Pyramids*. She has written two feature films "Lost and Delirious" and "Perfect Pie" as well as television movies and radio drama. Her work has enjoyed great success internationally. She is professor of drama at the University of Guelph, and currently lives with her husband and five children in Toronto.